I am proud to have been born in Nottinghamshire, the county whose fertile soils nurtured the acorn that grew into the mighty Major Oak. The county capital, the city of Nottingham, is the Jewel in the Crown of the East Midlands, a city of such magnificence that it merits not one, but two professional football teams. The county is a source of pride to anyone who hails from there and that is why I was honoured when asked to provide a foreword for this book, a tribute to a great province.

And on poring over the manuscript, my pride in my Nottinghamshire heritage grew to unparalleled proportions. When I read that HRH Queen Victoria crossed Trent Bridge in 1840, a lump came to my throat. My bottom lip trembled visibly on learning that Sutton-in-Ashfield is the home of Europe's largest sundial. And when I discovered that the Pet Shop Boys' Neil Tennant wrote West End Girls in the village of West Leake, I'm not ashamed to say that I cried like a baby.

So read on and learn things about your county that will swell your heart and leave the unfortunate inhabitants of lesser counties like Derbyshire and Leicestershire, green with envy.

Graham Dury

Co Editor, Viz Comic

INTRODUCTION

The origins of this book were born out of verbal jousting between Martin Goddard and Chris Adams. They were trying to 'outfact' each other on the subject of Nottinghamshire.

Nottingham has a long and important history much of which is both well documented and well known. There are also many famous personalities who are associated with the county, and their stories are easily accessible. This ensures that their importance as national and international figures is properly recognised and we are, of course, immensely proud of their achievements.

However, there are many stories which are less well known and some which have not been told at all. The aim of this book is to shine a light on some of these and in doing so to highlight many achievements and extraordinary events which have taken place here but which may not have been given due recognition.

In this book there are 301 Nottinghamshire facts some of which you might find surprising, which have shaped the county, its people and in some cases the world. We fully expect some of these to be known to many, but we hope that there will be something which surprises everybody.

Most facts are very clear and demonstrable but in a few rare cases, it has been difficult to establish a full and complete historical provenance. However, we have not included any material for which there is no supporting evidence. If we stimulate a debate and bring wider recognition to Nottingham and Nottinghamshire in the process so much the better.

We hope that you enjoy reading and discussing the wonderful stories which follow, and join with us in celebrating the lives of those who have made such a huge contribution to our county's rich heritage.

Chris Adams and Martin Goddard

301
amazing · rare · funny
NOTTINGHAMSHIRE
FACTS

Contents

1. Creswell Crags near Whitwell is the site of the only known Paleolithic cave art in the UK. Limestone engravings of bison, birds and other animals have been dated back at least 12,800 years (around the end of the last Ice Age), making them the most northerly cave art in Europe.

Creswell Crags Visitors Centre is home to many fascinating archeological finds and interesting exhibitions.

2. Sutton-in-Ashfield's town centre is home to the largest sundial in Europe.

3. Nottingham is unique in having two silver maces carried in its processions which dates back to the time when it had both a Saxon and a Norman borough. Until 1835, two sheriffs and two coroners were elected each year, and until the 17th century the Market Square had a dividing wall to separate the Anglo-Saxon and Norman communities. A metal line can still be seen in the new market square where the wall was. It was only because Edward I didn't want to pay for two lots of administration that the two towns were eventually amalgamated!

4. Wollaton Hall was built on the profits of coal between 1580 and 1588 at a cost estimated at £80,000. Try and convert that into today's money. Tradition asserts that it has 365 windows and 52 doors. The greenhouse, or Camellia House, was one of the first wrought iron buildings in the UK. Wollaton wagonway or 'rayled' line is attributed to be the first tracked railway in the world. Constructed of wooden tracks, it was built between 1603 and 1604 to connect Wollaton and Strelley coal mines.

5. In 1290, during the reign of Edward I, the English Parliament sat at Clipstone. The Normans established a hunting lodge there, which Henry I had enclosed into a park in 1180 (later enlarged by Edward III). The area was actually visited by every English monarch from Henry II to Richard II at some time or another. Tradition has it that it was even the meeting place of Richard I and Robin Hood.

6. Next time you walk past the old Nat West Bank building on the corner of Pelham Street and Thurland Street, look up. Perched by the brick chimneys on the Thurland Street side, you'll see a carved monkey. Allegedly a Victorian slang term for a mortgage, it's one of several jokes architect Watson Fothergill incorporated into the design of the bank, and indeed many of his buildings. Step inside and you'll see more monkeys, owls and even a pig – try and work that one out!

7. The original Theatre Royal once stood on St. Mary's Gate. It was opened in 1760 and led a colourful life before finally closing its doors in 1867.

On several occasions, police officers were apt to assault members of the audience who refused to remove their hats for the National Anthem. A popular venue for Byron, its greatest triumph was the visit of Edmund

Kean in 1861 to perform Hamlet. In 1995, the Kean's Head pub was opened in recognition of the occasion.

8. On the approach avenue to Vimy Ridge Farm near Kinoulton you'll find yourself flanked by 184 Lombardy Poplar trees lining the track. That they're reminiscent of the landscape of Belgium and northern France is no coincidence. They were planted by the farm's former owner, Sir Jessie (William Hinde), to commemorate the death of his son, Lt. Francis Montague Hinde, and those of his comrades at the Battle of the Somme in 1916. Each tree represents one trooper from the Sherwood Foresters Regiment who lost his life during the battle. Sir Jessie later started a scheme at the farm to train 200 ex-servicemen in agriculture, helping them to find work in a land fit for heroes.

9. Not altogether unrelated, one of the first municipal car parks outside London was opened in 1933 on land near Huntingdon Street. The aim was to provide work for disabled war veterans, who dressed resplendently in a chauffeur-style uniform. Spaces for 80 cars were provided at the very reasonable fee of one shilling all day.

10. Oak from Sherwood Forest was used in the reconstruction of St. Paul's Cathedral after the Great Fire of London in 1666.

11. Stapleford is home to a unique Anglo-Saxon Cross, dating back almost as far as the Viking invasion. Carved sometime between 680 and 780 AD, it's thought to be the oldest Christian memorial in the Midlands. Its survival is amazing for it has been moved twice, and now resides in St. Helen's churchyard.

12. The Pilgrim Fathers were from the Worksop area. Scrooby postmaster, William Brewster and Babworth parson, Richard Clyfton, were both Separatists who believed in freedom of worship and religious tolerance. Fleeing Britain in fear of their lives after having found themselves at odds with the Crown, they initially sailed for Holland, but danger followed them. So in 1620 they crossed the Atlantic in the Mayflower to found Plymouth, Massachusetts – one of the earliest English settlements in North America and the origin of the American tradition of Thanksgiving.

The state flag of Pennsylvania hangs inside Oxton Church. It was presented to the church in 1951 by the State Governor in memory of the sons of Oxton who sailed with William Penn in 1682 to found the colony.

13. The original Trent Bridge was built in 924, and until the mid-18th century there was no other bridge over the Trent upstream nearer than Swarkestone in Derbyshire. It was known as the 'Heth Beth Bridge', which probably meant bridge by the hythe (or wharf) near the beth (or ford). Around 1156, Henry II replaced it with a grander structure that contained a chapel to St. Mary.

In 1840 Queen Victoria crossed the bridge, which explains why it carries the Royal Coat of Arms.

The current bridge was designed by a Mr. Tarbotton in 1871 and unveiled to strong criticism that it was far wider than it would ever need to be – yet 55 years later its width had to be nearly doubled!

14. Nottingham's favourite meeting point, the Council House steps, are flanked by two stone art-deco styled lions. Here you can spot many a nervous first date. Created by Joseph Else they are titled 'Meneleus and Agamemnon'. The popular names are 'Leo and Oscar'.

15. Portland stone used for the Council House came from the Isle of Purbeck in Dorset. The quarry was first opened for the building of St. Paul's Cathedral.

16. Watnall has always been associated with weather reports (BBC forecaster Jack Scott worked there for a time) but until the early 1960s it was the location of RAF Watnall, which surprisingly had no airfield. It was built in great secrecy as a fighter command HQ during the Second World War, and was the control and administration centre for 12 Group Fighter Command. Their commander was Air Chief Marshall Sir Trafford Leigh-Mallory, who lived at Woodborough Hall at the time. His brother, George Mallory, was the adventurer who died attempting to climb Everest. Although Watnall had no airfield, it did have a series of underground bunkers, which became part of the top secret ROTOR (radar systems) network in the 1950s and 60s, guarding the country against potential hostile attacks by Russia. It tracked aircraft movement until it was closed in 1961.

17. Some would say the finest avenue of trees in England can be found in Clumber Park near Worksop. The three-mile stretch of lime trees is the longest in Europe – some 1,296 trees in total.

18. The original St. Pancras Station clock which is 18ft high, is now located on a barn wall end in Thurgaton. After being dismantled in the 1970s, it was sold to a collector. Unfortunately it was accidentally dropped and smashed into many pieces. Mr Hoggard, who then worked as a train guard, was able to retrieve all the pieces, and over the next few years, painstakingly restore the clock. The clock's design was used as the basis for a replica to be produced for the refurbished St. Pancras International Station.

19. Newcastle House, once the home of Viyella, is a splendid art deco office building on Castle Boulevard. It has a unique chiming bell system with a different song for each day of the week. From Monday to Friday the bells play 'Bobby Shafto', 'Oranges and Lemons', 'British Grenadiers', 'The Ash Grove', and 'Frere Jacques'. On Saturday they play 'All Through The Night' and on Sunday 'Vicar of Bray'. They can even be adjusted to play Christmas carols.

20. The George Hotel (now the Mercure Hotel) on George Street can boast several claims to fame over the years. Charles Dickens stayed there in 1852 and the cheque signed by his business agent is still on display. It was the site of the founding of Notts County Football Club and more recently Richard Burton, Elizabeth Taylor and Quentin Tarantino have graced its rooms.

CHARLES DICKENS
STAYED HERE
24th AUGUST 1852

THE DICKENS FELLOWSHIP
NOTTINGHAM BRANCH

Commemorating The Formation Of
The Oldest League Club In The World

Notts County Football Club

In The George IV Room
In 1862
At This Hotel

21. The Black Boy Hotel was also a favourite of the stars, including Laurence Olivier and Gregory Peck. It was also used regularly by the Australian cricket team. It was demolished in the late 60s and has been much missed ever since.

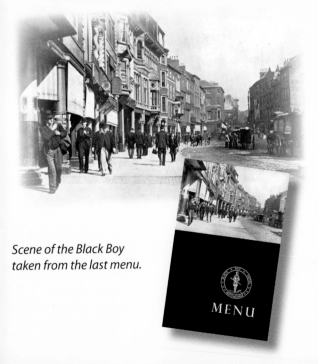

Scene of the Black Boy taken from the last menu.

MENU

22. Eastwood's Sun Inn was the birthplace of the Midland Railway in 1832.

23. King's Mill Hospital, Sutton-In-Ashfield, founded in 1942, was the first US Army hospital in England. Notable visitors included James Stewart and Clark Gable who narrowly escaped serious injury on one of his bombing missions, when shrapnel sliced through the heel of his boot!

24. The Park Estate in Nottingham is said to have the largest gas street-lighting system in Europe. The private estate chose to remain lit by gas in 1937 when the rest of Nottingham's street lighting was converted to electricity. There are reckoned to be 220 lamp-posts across the estate, giving off an atmospheric soft white glow which is quite unique.

25. Since 1822 a narrow door tucked among the crowded streets of Angel Row has been the entrance to one of Nottingham's lesser known historic institutions. It was built in 1752 as a town house for George Smith, a successful Nottingham banker. The house was subsequently purchased by Nottingham Subscription Library and is now the home of Bromley House Library. Across the floor of one of the first floor rooms known as the Standfast Room is a rare meridian dial consisting of a brass strip, with a fine line engraved on it. It was laid down in about 1834 to aid the telling of the correct time by observing the transit of the spot of sunlight across the meridian at local solar noon in Nottingham.

26. Thoresby Hall in north Notts has a number of unusual follies. One particular folly is dedicated to Spencer Perceval. In 1812, he became the only PM to have been assassinated in the House of Commons. Another folly, Nelson's Pyramid, commemorates the first and the second Earl of Manvers who both served in the Napoleonic War sea campaigns.

Thoresby Hall

Battle of the Nile memorial

Nelson's Pyramid

27. Notts County is the oldest professional football club in the world. Formed in 1862 at the George Hotel in Nottingham, now the Mercure Inn, where a commemorative plaque celebrates the event. It is believed that they probably adopted their famous black-and-white-striped shirts from the Nottingham High School colours. They are considered to be one of the pioneers of the modern game, and were founder members of the Football League in 1888 – which didn't stop them ending the first season 11th place out of 12!

28. The Forest Recreation Ground was once home to Nottingham Racecourse. With an impressive grandstand built in 1777, the venue was known to draw crowds of over 15,000. Racing was held from the late 17th to the late 19th century, when it moved to Colwick.

29. In 1771, one of the first recorded cricket matches was played on the Forest Racecourse where huge crowds of over 20,000 gathered. Thousands of pounds were wagered on the outcome of the match.

30. The Forest Recreation Ground was also the first home of the newly formed Forest Football Club (as it was then known). They started out playing 'shinty' (a form of hockey originating from Scotland), and went on to play their matches on the ground for 14 years. A special service was held at St. Andrew's Church on Mansfield Road in 1965 to celebrate 100 years of the club.

Nottingham Forest founded in 1865 at the Clinton Arms Hotel now The Orange Tree.

31. Forest's first match against Notts County in 1866 was the beginning of the longest contested local club rivalry in the world. It was recorded that Forest fielded 17 men to County's 11 and allegedly won 1- 0 with a touchdown! Other records show a 0 - 0 stalemate.

32. Nottingham Forest can claim several footballing innovations. They were the first club to use shin guards (being invented by Forest captain Samuel Widdowson in 1874), involved in the first match to utilise a referee's whistle in 1878, the first to use a crossbar instead of tape, the first to use goal nets, and also pioneers in floodlighting.

33. Celebrity Forest supporters include James Dean Bradfield of the Manic Street Preachers, Kenneth Clark MP, golfer Lee Westwood, Deep Purple drummer Ian Paice, boxing champion Carl Froch, Olympic skaters Jayne Torvill and Christopher Dean, Portugal manager Luiz Felipe Scolari, former Blue Peter presenter Richard Bacon, Coronation Street's Steve McDonald and the late Ted Moult – who appeared as the guest supporter for the Forest team on the BBC Quiz Ball competition during the 1967/68 season.

34. Forest are the only club to have played teams from all four home countries in the FA Cup. Linfield (1888/9 2-2 replay to be in Belfast but Linfield scratched from the competition) Queens Park (1884/85 lost 0-3 in semi final replay in Edinburgh) Cardiff City 1922 and Wrexham 1982. It was the only time an FA Cup semi-final has been played outside England or Wales.

35. Forest hold the accolade of the highest away win in the FA Cup, with a 14-0 whitewash at Clapton on 17th January 1891.

36. Elton John`s uncle, Roy Dwight, played for Forest when they won the FA Cup in 1959. Dwight broke his leg but could not be substituted as it was not allowed at that time. Forest had to play on with ten men.

37. In 1886 Joseph Bates, manager of New Basford machine builders Swift and Wass – and a keen Forest amateur – moved to London to work for the Woolwich Arsenal gun factory, which was setting up a works' team. After writing to his home club for donations, he received a bundle of Forest shirts, and the red and white strip of Arsenal FC was born. Forest also donated shirts to a formative Liverpool FC. Today, whenever Forest play Arsenal, Forest are given the choice of which colours to play in, regardless of whether they are at home. This is done in recognition of this historic connection. The red colour Forest wear was inspired by Garibaldi, the founder of modern Italy.

38. Not to be outdone, Notts County lent their own colours to the mighty Juventus. From the late 1890s, Juventus played in a cheap pink kit, pink being the only material available, but because the colours kept fading they asked English player John Savage if he had any contacts back home who could source something better suited to the wash. Originally they were going to import kits in the red of Nottingham Forest, but a mix-up meant they got County's black and white instead!

39. Bertie Mee, manager of the famous double-winning Arsenal team of the early 1970s, was born in Bulwell and played much of his early football in the area including a stint at Mansfield Town.

40. Gedling churchyard is the resting place of two of cricket's great figures: bowler Alfred Shaw and batsman Arthur Shrewsbury who played in the 1870s and 1880s. The batsman and the bowler competed with each other each other while they were alive and it is ironic that they were buried a wicket's length apart.

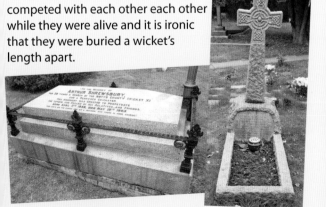

It was said Shaw could drop the ball on a shilling, which might not be too far-fetched. During a dazzling career he bowled more overs than he conceded runs and never bowled a wide or a no-ball. He also became the first bowler to dismiss 2,000 batsmen in first-class cricket, clean bowling W.G. Grace 20 times along the way. On March 15th 1877, at the Melbourne Cricket Ground Australia, the first ball of what was the first international cricket match and therefore the first ever Test match between England and Australia (a series that was later to become known as 'the Ashes') was bowled by Alfred Shaw of Burton Joyce to Charles Bannerman.

During his time, Shrewsbury was widely recognised as England's leading batsman. When W.G. Grace was asked his ideal opening partner for the England XI, he replied: 'Give me Arthur!' During his career, Shaw scored over 26,000 runs, including ten double centuries and 49 centuries.

41. Champion bare-knuckle prize fighter William 'Bendigo' Thompson (1811-1880) was born and lived in Nottingham. Legendary for his mid-fight acrobatics and colourful insults, he amassed an enormous fan base during his lifetime (Sir Arthur Conan Doyle once called him 'The Pride of Nottingham'). In 1845 a fierce rivalry with Hucknall's Ben Caunt led one fight to a staggering 96 rounds! He died at his home in Beeston and his lion-shaped tombstone rests in St. Mary's Cemetery, Sneinton. He is one of the few athletes whose name is borne by a city - Bendigo in Australia.

42. Bulwell's William Murray was voted Britain's Perfect Man in 1901. It was the first event in a competition now known as Mr Universe (among the judges was Sir Arthur Conan Doyle!) One of Murray's most famous appearances came in 1894 when he successfully fought a lion in San Francisco!

43. You wouldn't know it, but in his day long-distance swimmer 'Torpedo' Tom Blower, from Hyson Green, was quite a national celebrity. Known for his astonishing endurance, he once undertook a 30 hour non-stop marathon at Sneinton's Victoria Baths – swimming 2,664 lengths or 55½ miles.

In 1937 he swam the English Channel in 13 hours 29 minutes, smashing the previous record by a phenomenal 23 minutes! In 1948 he joined the very short list of people to have swum the English Channel both ways.

He was also the first person to swim the Northern Irish Sea in 1949. He died in 1955 and is buried in Bulwell Cemetery.

44. Local mechanic and aviator Bob Slack made flying history in 1912 with a 1,000 mile trip around Britain. He then added to it by flying from Paris to London, becoming the first man to fly newspapers between the two cities.

45. The King's Cup Air Race, which was established in 1922, became the world's longest-running major air race series. In 1967 it was held at Tollerton Aerodrome in Nottingham. It returned to Nottingham in 1968, and a third and final time in 1970.

46. During the 1893/4 season, Notts County became the first second division club (now the Championship) to win the FA Cup.

47. World-famous mountaineer Doug Scott was born in Nottingham in 1941. He holds the record for the first ascent of the south-west face of Mount Everest, and was also the first Briton to conquer the mountain. He has completed over 45 expeditions to inner Asia reaching the summit of 40 peaks of which half were first ascents. Doug is considered to be one of the world's leading high altitude and big wall climbers.

48. In January 2003, 23 year-old Andrew Cooney, from the small Nottinghamshire village of Thurgarton, became the youngest person to trek the 703 miles from the Antarctic coast to the South Pole. The trip took Cooney to altitudes of 9,000 feet in temperatures of 52 degrees below zero and was completed in 53 days.
Also from Thurgarton, Fiona Thornewill broke the record for walking solo and unaided to the South Pole. She achieved her success on 28th January 2004 after 42 days on the ice. There she met her husband Mike, who had travelled to the Pole with five companions following in the tracks of Sir Ernest Shackleton`s trek which had taken place more than a century earlier. It is most unusual that such a small village should produce three modern arctic adventurers.

49. Famous 'Bentley Boy' Sir Henry 'Tim' Birkin was born into a wealthy Nottingham lace family in 1896. He ultimately inherited the family business and much of its wealth was spent on developing the supercharged Blower Bentley. Of the Bentley Boys, Birkin was the one the schoolboys knew best. He triumphed at the Le Mans 24 Hour in 1929 in a 6.6 litre Bentley Six Speed, and again in 1931. He died at the age of 36 from blood poisoning after burning his arm on the exhaust pipe of a Maserati he'd been driving.

50. Harold Larwood (1904-1995) and Bill Voce (1919-1984) were Nottinghamshire men who bowled for Notts CCC and England. Larwood was born in Nuncargate, a village south of Kirkby-in-Ashfield, and Voce in Annesley Woodhouse. Both achieved infamy for their parts in the famous 'bodyline' series against Australia. The test matches were so controversial that both men were omitted from the next Test team to face Australia. Voce died in Lenton and Larwood died in Sydney, Australia having retired there following his playing career. Larwood has a commemorative plaque on the pavilion in Nuncargate, and his name is also on display in Sydney Harbour .

Larwood's statue in Kirkby-in-Ashfield

51. Stuart Pearce captained Nottingham Forest for nearly ten years, winning 78 England caps along the way. His success may have come as a surprise to

Pearce himself, for when he joined the club he was so unsure of his future there he advertised his services as an electrician in the match programme. Brian Clough even brought him a kettle to fix!

52. Born in Nottingham in the 1960s, Forest stalwart Viv Anderson was the first black player to be capped for England when they played Czechoslovakia in 1978.

53. Graham Taylor, who managed the England football team between 1990 and 1993, was born in Worksop. His England tenure was not a great success but his league management of Watford and Aston Villa football clubs were more impressive.

54. Trent Bridge is the third oldest major cricket ground in the UK. It was founded in 1838 by the landlord of the Bell Inn, William Clarke. Competitive county cricket was first played there in 1840 against Sussex, and the first Test Match followed in 1899. The Trent Bridge Pavilion was the largest in England when it was built in 1886. During World War I it was used as a military hospital, and during World War II as the Army's central mail sorting office.

Trent Bridge also has a history of hosting football matches. Notts County played their important games there in the 1860s, moving there permanently between 1883 and 1910. It has even hosted an international football match, with England beating Ireland 6-0 on February 20th 1897.

55. Notts CCC have won the County Championship six times since the turn of the 20th century; 1907, 1929, 1981, 1987, 2005 and 2010. On five occasions when Notts won the Championship, England went on to win the Ashes!

56. The old Nottingham Ice Stadium hosted a golden age of boxing from the 1940s to the 1970s. A prestigious venue with a national reputation, it saw over 40 major championship fights and 10 title eliminator fights during its tenure. Henry Cooper, Chris Finnegan, Jim Watt, Alan Rudkin, Jack Bodell and John Conteh all fought bouts at the stadium. It was also the venue for the fastest British title fight finish on record when Dave Charnley stopped Darkie Hughes in an amazing 40 seconds in 1961.

57. The Robin Hood Marathon has been voted Number Two Marathon in the UK by readers of Runners Weekly. It began in 1981 as one of many marathons supported by former Olympian Chris Brasher, and still attracts more than 12,000 entrants every year.

58. The North Nottinghamshire Village of Letwell was the site of the first St. Ledger horse race, which was run on a farm on the Langold Estate in 1776.

59. Gunn & Moore, two of the most historic names in cricket, trace their origins back to William Gunn who we believe co-founded the business in 1885 with local business man Thomas James Moore. The business produces 35,000 bats a year. Gunn played football for Forest and Notts County winning two England caps. His uncle played in the first Ashes test at Trent Bridge. Over the years many England players have used Gunn & Moore bats.

60. Nottingham Rugby Club played at Ireland Avenue in Beeston for over a century, only vacating the ground at the end of the 2005/6 season. Until 1929 the changing rooms were in the nearby Victoria Hotel where both teams had to share a single bath in the stables. Much later the club made history in 1987 when they played in the inaugural match of the Courage Club Championship, which changed rugby from a sport of friendlies into a competitive league competition. Nottingham beat Moseley 21-12.

61. Field Mill, the home of Mansfield Town FC, is regarded as one of the oldest football grounds in the world. Football has been played there since 1861.

62. Nottinghamshire Cricket Club are the only county club to have had its players go on strike. In the summer of 1881 the club protested over pay and benefits. It wasn't until the following season that the strike was satisfactorily settled.

63. When Nottingham Forest first won the FA Cup in 1898, the practice was to take photographs of both teams with the trophy before the game while the players' kits were still clean. The photographer in 1898 was concerned that Forest's red shirts wouldn't suit the picture, so he photographed them in their opponent's kit. Forest went on to lift the trophy and pictures of the victorious side show them in Derby shirts.

64. Tinsley Lindley was born in Nottingham in 1865. He played football for several clubs including Notts County, but made his name with Nottingham Forest through various FA Cup exploits in the 1880s.

Alongside Sam Widdowson he was the epitome of the gentleman amateur, preferring to play in walking brogues as he thought football boots affected his sprinting speed. He also captained England, scoring on his debut and his next eight matches – a feat that remains unequalled today.

Lindley also played rugby for Nottingham RFC and cricket for Notts CCC, and went on to practice Law, serving as a County Court Judge.

He stayed loyal to Forest, serving on the club committee for several years. He was awarded an OBE in 1918, and died in Nottingham in 1940, aged 74.

65. Arguably the most famous chime in the world comes from a bell named after a Nottingham man by the name of Caunt. Champion bare knuckle boxer Ben Caunt came from Hucknall, and is buried in Hucknall churchyard. He was a huge man with a big voice and a booming laugh. He retired from boxing in 1857 at the age of 42, and later became a publican in St. Martins Lane, London. Former MP, Mr George Caunt, discovered in parliamentary papers that the 14.5-tonne bell Big Ben was so-called after Ben Caunt and his booming voice (though the bell was never officially named).

66. Muhammad Ali 'the greatest' has visited Nottingham on several occasions. He first appeared for a few days at the Nottingham Ice stadium to promote his forthcoming fight with Henry Cooper at

Wembley stadium in June 1963. Cassius Clay, as he was then known, won the fight when it was stopped in the fifth round. Ali returned to Nottingham in 1992 to sign copies of his official biography at Dillons book shop which was then on Wheeler Gate. The queues stretched to the Old Market Square.

67. Steve Hodge, the former Forest midfield star, owns the most famous or infamous football shirt; now known as 'The hand of God' shirt. He acquired it from Diego Maradona when he swapped shirts after the controversial World Cup quarter final match in 1986 between Argentina and England.

68. Matt Smith, the actor who took on the roll of Dr. Who in 2009 played for Nottingham Forest as a member of the youth team. He played alongside Jermaine Jenas and others. Matt is a huge Stuart Pearce fan. His grandfather played for Notts County.

69. Nottingham lace-maker Herbert Kilpin, a butcher's son born in Nottingham on 28 January 1870, grew up with nine brothers and sisters at 129 Mansfield Road. In his late twenties he emigrated to Milan to work in the textile industry. After a heavy drinking session in a Milanese tavern, the homesick Kilpin and five friends decided to start a football team to remind them of home: thus AC Milan was born.

Kilpin became the club's first coach and captain, as well as the team's star player. Without him AC Milan's glorious trophy-laden history may not have happened.

70. Accomplished portrait painter Dame Laura Knight was born in Long Eaton and attended the Nottingham College of Art from 1889. She was famous for her paintings of ballet and the circus, and was official artist at the Nuremberg war crime trials.

Dame Laura Knight, artist, lived here (1877~1970)

71. Alan Sillitoe was born and bred in Lenton, penning ground-breaking novels such as 'Saturday Night and Sunday Morning' and 'Loneliness of the Long Distance Runner'. Many of his characters were based on local people he knew.

72. Mansfield-born painter James Collinson was a founding member of the artistic Pre-Raphaelite Brotherhood in 1848, and was even engaged to poet Christina Rossetti for a time. As a devout Catholic he decided to abandon art (and Rossetti) for a life of celibacy and prayer. You can take a look at his work in the Nottingham Castle Museum.

73. Mary Gillick (1881-1965) was born in Nottingham and studied at the Girls' High School and School of Art. She produced the first uncrowned portrait of the Queen which featured on the new coinage introduced in 1953, and went on to be used until 1967 on all pre-decimal coins.

74. Artist Richard Parkes Bonnington was born in 1802 in Arnold and spent his early years in Nottingham. The Wallace Collection in London displays many of his paintings, but you can also see his work in Nottingham's Castle Museum. He died aged 26 of tuberculosis on September 23rd 1828.

75. Author Graham Greene started out with a career in journalism at the Nottingham Daily Journal. He lived just off Sherwood Rise and later moved to Forest Fields. It was also while in the city that he joined the Roman Catholic church. The 1936 novel 'A Gun for Sale' is set in a town loosely based on Nottingham called 'Nottwich'

76. Geoffrey Trease (1909-1998) wrote over 100 books for children and adults. He also produced his own 'British Boys Magazine' and won the New York Tribune award for his non-fiction work 'This is Your Century'. He was also highly regarded in the old Soviet Union where his novel, based on Robin Hood, 'Bows Against the Barons' sold over 100,000 copies.

The Trease family business on Castle Gate Nottingham

77. Helen Cresswell (1935 - 2005) famous for children's stories such as 'The Bongleweed', 'The Piemakers' and much-loved characters like Lizzie Dripping, was born and educated in Eakring.

78. Following his death in France in 1930, D. H. Lawrence's headstone was transported to England and is now on display in his hometown library of Eastwood.

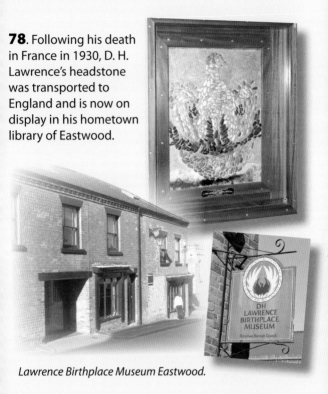

Lawrence Birthplace Museum Eastwood.

79. In Ian Fleming's James Bond novel 'Thunderball' there is a whole section on Nottingham Castle. '...that extraordinary trademark of a doll's house swimming in chocolate fudge with Nottingham Castle written underneath...'

Nottingham Castle is a 17th Century Ducal Palace, now an art gallery and museum, built on the foundations of the original medieval castle.

80. Peter Pan author JM Barrie began a career in journalism at the Nottingham Journal. It's rumoured that Peter Pan was inspired by a Nottingham street urchin, and Barry wrote his classic children's story at his lodgings in 5 Birkland Avenue (1883-4) near the Arboretum Park which could have been his inspiration for Neverland.

81. Celebrated crime writer and University of Nottingham alumnus John Harvey is the author behind the Charlie Resnick detective books which are actually set in the Canning Circus area. One of his works of fiction 'Lonely Hearts' has been voted into the Sunday Times top 100 crime novels of the century.

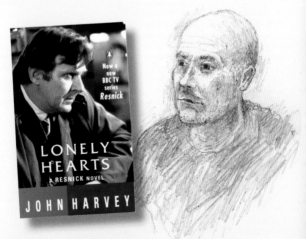

Early copy of Resnick novel
Cover featuring Hollywood Star Tom Wilkinson

82. Weary Willie and Tired Tim from the comic Chips were created by Nottingham cartoonist and illustrator Tom Browne. These two lovable tramps featured on the front page of the comic for over 50 years. He also created the character for the Johnnie Walker whisky brand.

83. If Dudley Dexter Watkins doesn't ring a bell, then Desperate Dan and Lord Snooty should! The Nottingham Guardian declared Watkins (who developed his talent at the Nottingham School of Art) a schoolboy genius. He illustrated the Boots Company Magazine 'Boots News' before he created and illustrated characters for the 'Dandy' and 'Beano'.

84. Thomas Henry Fisher, born in 1879 at Eastwood Nottinghamshire, is the illustrator behind Richmal Crompton's 'Just William' books. Fisher also used to work for the 'Nottingham Football Post' as well as 'Punch'.

85. Mario Armengol was a refugee from the Spanish Civil War who was based in Laneham, near Retford, during the Second World War. Mario was commissioned by the Ministry of Information to produce what became a series of famous Second World War propaganda cartoons.

86. J.R.R. Tolkien's Aunt Jane Neave may have been the person on whom he based the Lord of the Rings character Gandalf. Tolkien visited his Aunt's farm in Gedling on several occasions while he was a student and later when he was in the army during the First World War. Her qualities of strength, physical presence and mystical tendencies are said to have greatly influenced the young Tolkien.

87. Stephen Lowe, Sneinton-born playwright and scriptwriter, was involved in the theatre from the age of 9. He had various jobs, including being a shepherd in North Yorkshire, before his big break came at the Nottingham Playhouse where his play 'Touched' was staged. He has written countless scripts such as 'Dalziel and Pascoe', 'Coronation Street' and other TV series.

88. Arthur Mee was born in Stapleford in 1875. He left school at 14 to join the Nottingham Evening Post, becoming Editor by the age of 20. Among his many published works he produced the first newspaper for children 'The Children's Newspaper', published until 1965, and 'The King's England', which was a guide to the English counties. He is probably best-known for the 'Children's Encyclopedia', which he founded and edited. It was published from 1908 to 1964 and could be found on the bookshelves of many families across the British Empire.

It's said that an edition of this work, from around 1908, is responsible for the myth that lemmings throw themselves off cliffs. That they do no such thing has not prevented this belief entering the public consciousness.

89. Samuel Bourne (1834-1912), a professional photographer from Nottingham, was one of the great pioneers of travel photography, particularly in his work in India and the Himalayas. His pictures may be seen at the India Record Office in London, and at the Royal Photographic Society in Bath England.

90. Former Nottingham policeman Nigel McCrery now writes for TV. His work includes 'Silent Witness' and 'Backup'. He was nominated for an Emmy for 'New Tricks'.

91. The Scarlet Pimpernel, originally a play by Baroness Emma Orczy, premiered at Nottingham's Theatre Royal on October 15th 1903. It was a resounding success and she published it as a novel in 1905.

92. Writer and playwright Willis Hall, who was married to the late Jill Bennett, settled in Nottingham in 1953. To give his work the right atmosphere he's known to have trained with Nottingham Forest when writing a play about a disabled footballer, and he spent several nights at Hyson Green police station before writing 'The Claverdon Road Job'. His other work includes 'Billy Liar', 'Whistle Down the Wind', and 'A Kind of Loving'.

93. Sir Walter Scott liked to stay at The Saracen's Head in Newark. In fact, fictional character Jeanie Deans also stayed there in Scott's classic novel 'Heart of Midlothian'.

94. Sudha Kheterpal, percussionist with Faithless, grew up in Nottingham and attended the Nottingham Girls High School.

95. Three Degrees singer and founder member Valerie Holiday lives in Arnold. She married life-long fan Jaghir Babra in 2002, though he was initially too nervous to ask for her autograph!

96. Alma Lucy Reville, Lady Hitchcock (1899-1982) was born in the St. Ann's area of Nottingham. A gifted editor and screenwriter, she developed a close bond with future husband Alfred Hitchcock while she was working as assistant director on one of his first films. When checking through the final cut of 'Psycho', Alma noticed a single blink of Janet Leigh's eye as she lay dead. The gaff was replaced with a cutaway shot.

97. Tom Baker, actor and erstwhile Dr Who, worked for local rose grower Harry Wheatcroft and also lived locally before he became a household name. He married Anna Wheatcroft in 1961, before leaving the area to begin his acting career.

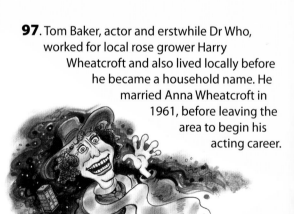

98. Infamous punk band the Sex Pistols' debut album 'Never Mind the Bollocks, Here's The Sex Pistols' featured in a famous case at Nottingham Crown Court in November 1977. The manager of Nottingham's Virgin Records was arrested and charged under the Indecent Advertising Act of 1898 for positioning copies of the album sleeve in the shop window.

John Mortimer QC, author of 'Rumpole of the Bailey', appeared for the defence. He called upon a professor of English from the University of Nottingham, James Kinsey, to explain the origins of the offending word. There was even a personal appearance from Johnny Rotten, before he was ushered out for trying to smoke in court!

NEVER MIND THE BOLLOCKS HERE'S THE **SEX PISTOLS**

99. It is well known that the Goose Fair is one of the biggest and most popular fairs in the country. Less known, however, is the fact that Madame Tussaud brought her travelling show of waxworks to the fair in 1819 and 1829, charging one shilling to view the display to pay off a contractual debt!

100. The Boat Club has become a Nottingham institution over the years. Situated by the banks of the River Trent it has featured some of the most famous and infamous bands in the world on its bill. A wooden display board in the main function room reveals a roll of honour that includes Jimi Hendrix, T-Rex, Elton John, Rod Stewart, Jeff Beck, Howlin' Wolf, John Lee Hooker, the Sex Pistols, Led Zeppelin and Black Sabbath.

The Boat Club (centre) rebuilt in 1913 after it was burnt down by the Suffragette Movement for being a men only club.

101. In 1867 the Music Hall star and male impersonator Vesta Tilley made her stage debut at St. George's Hall in Nottingham at the tender age of three. Danmark House in Gedling was originally commissioned by a former prince of Denmark for the star.

102. Robin Bailey (1919–1999) was born in Hucknall. He's probably best known for his role as Judge Graves in the TV series 'Rumpole of the Bailey' and Uncle Mort in 'I Didn't Know You Cared'.

103. The Andy Williams Fan Club was first started in Nottingham's Park estate.

104. Tommy Steel made his stage debut at the Nottingham Empire Theatre of Varieties in November 1956. Ken Dodd also made his first professional performance at the Empire back in 1954.

105. Laurel and Hardy were regular visitors to Bottesford, staying at the Bull Inn where the licensee, Olga Healey, was Stan's sister. They first stayed while appearing at the Nottingham Empire Theatre in 1952.

106. There is a detached house in a Nottingham suburb with a huge garage which was commissioned by Freddie Mercury, so that he could park his Rolls Royce when he came to visit his sister.

107. Bruce Dickinson, lead singer with heavy metal legends Iron Maiden, hails from Worksop. When he's not performing with his band he often works as a commercial pilot captaining passenger aircraft. He also flies the band around in their own plane 'Ed Force 1'.

108. Paul McCartney and Wings played their first ever concert at Nottingham University Students' Union on Wednesday 9th February 1972. Tickets cost 40p. It was the first time McCartney had performed on stage in five years. He only decided to return to gigging on a

109. Nile Rodgers and Bernard Edwards decided to form the band Chic at the Bentinck Hotel on Carrington Street after backing a little known US soul singer at the Heart of the Midlands (later Rock City) in the 1970s.

110. Virtuoso guitarist Alvin Lee, famous for bands such as the Jaybirds and Ten Years After, was born in Nottingham. His performance with the latter at Woodstock remains a standard for guitarists to this day.

111. Graeme Park, the pioneering house music DJ and radio broadcaster, began his career selling vinyl records in Nottingham's Selectadisc. He began DJing when Selectadisc's owner decided to open a club called 'The Garage' and 'Graeme' was his choice for DJ. From there he progressed to the legendary Hacienda nightclub in Manchester. He is often credited as the 'Father of

House', and remains a popular radio presenter.

112. Deep Purple drummer Ian Paice was born in Linfield Road on the Broxtowe Estate in 1948. Pete York, drummer with the Spencer Davis Group attended Nottingham High School and Trent College.

113. Neil Tennant wrote the Pet Shop Boys' song West End Girls in West Leake while staying with his cousin.

114. Nottingham band KWS achieved worldwide success in 1993 with 'Please Don't Go', reaching number one in the UK and the United States. The band dedicated the song to Forest legend Des Walker who was about to leave the club for Sampdoria in Italy.

115. Influential broadcaster and Notts County fan, Trevor Dann, was educated at the Nottingham High School. Beginning his career at Radio Nottingham, Dann went on to work at Radio 1, BBC 2's Old Grey Whistle Test and produced 1985's Live Aid, for which he won a BAFTA. In 1988 he helped found radio station GLR, thereby launching Chris Evans' and Danny Baker's careers. He also produced the now-defunct 'Top of the Pops' from 1996–2000.

116. Billy Ivory proudly hails from Southwell. Originally a binman, his first major role was in Coronation Street as Eddie Ramsden. He has since penned some of the great TV dramas. His first piece for TV, 'Journey to Knock', was based on his mother who died of motor neurone disease and won Best Screenplay, Best Actor and Best Drama at the 1992 European Television Awards in Rheims. His subsequent work has included 'Common as Muck', 'A Thing Called Love', 'The Invisibles' and 'Bomber's Moon'.

117. Barry Howard of Hi De Hi fame was raised in St. Ann's. His parents owned a shop on St. Ann's Well Road.

118. Michael Crawford lived in Nottingham during the early 1960s, before he became a household name. He was a regular performer at the Playhouse, and appeared in the opening season of 'The Importance of Being Earnest' as Algernon Moncrief.

119. Founder Stereo MC's members Rob Birch and Nick Hallam hail from Ruddington.

120. Born on 27 September 1944 in Muswell Hill in London, Bernard William Jewry better known as Alvin Stardust moved at an early age to Mansfield. He was famous for the hits 'My Jealous Mind' and 'My Coo-Ca-Choo'. He taught himself to play the guitar by ear at 12 and originally came to fame as Shane Fenton with Shane Fenton and the Fentones. He was a boarder at Southwell Minster Grammar School.

121. Worksop lad John Parr co-wrote the album 'Bad Attitude' with Meat Loaf. He wrote the themes to 'Three Men and a Baby', 'The Running Man', and the lyrics to the film theme and successful chart song 'St. Elmo's Fire', for which he received a Grammy nomination.

122. Composer Eric Coates (1886-1957) was born in Hucknall. He wrote many musical works, including 'The Dam Busters March' and 'Sleepy Lagoon', which is the theme to Desert Island Discs.

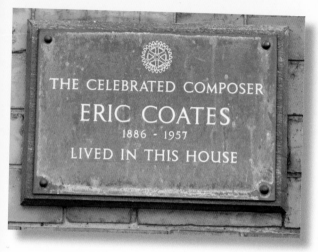

THE CELEBRATED COMPOSER
ERIC COATES
1886 - 1957
LIVED IN THIS HOUSE

123. Inventor of the cream-pie-in-the-face gag Fred Westcott (1866-1941), better-known by the stage name Fred Karno, lived on Coalpit Lane in Nottingham. Debuting as an acrobat at the Crown and Cushion on Fletcher Gate (Nottingham's oldest music hall - 1740) he went on to become one of the greatest impressarios and showmen in the world. He discovered Charlie Chaplin and mentored Stan Laurel under what became known as 'Fred Karno's Army'. He later acquired a houseboat on the Thames, which is now owned by David Gilmour of Pink Floyd and contains a recording studio where many of the band's famous works were recorded.

124. Printer's son Robert Harris was born and brought up in Sherwood, Nottingham. Erstwhile Political Editor of The Observer, Sunday Times columnist and Panorama reporter, Harris is also the multi-million best selling author of the novels 'Fatherland', 'Enigma' and 'Archangel'. He also wrote 'Selling Hitler', which was made into a film starring Alan Bennett, Tom Baker, Alexei Sayle and Richard Wilson.

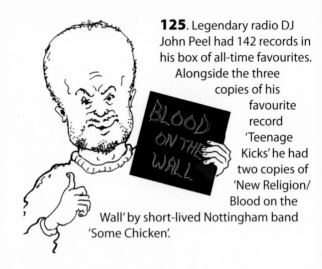

125. Legendary radio DJ John Peel had 142 records in his box of all-time favourites. Alongside the three copies of his favourite record 'Teenage Kicks' he had two copies of 'New Religion/ Blood on the Wall' by short-lived Nottingham band 'Some Chicken'.

126. Actor Donald Pleasance (1919-1995) was from Worksop. His role as the POW forger in The Great Escape had more than a ring of truth as he was an RAF POW during the Second World War, and produced and acted in plays while captive. He played archetypal James Bond villain Blofeld (parodied by Mike Myers' Dr Evil) and also Dr Loomis in the Halloween series.

127. Clifton-born artist Graham Dury has been drawing the controversial Viz cartoon characters for over twenty years since graduating in Botany from The University Nottingham in 1984. Characters created by Dury include Spoilt Bastard, Biffa Bacon and the Fat Slags.

128. Cantamus, a girl's choir from Mansfield, has won 21 first prizes in international choral competitions including the world choir championships 'the Choir Olympics' in 2004 and 2006.

129. Alan Sytner is well-known for founding successful prestige car dealer Sytners on Carlton Hill. Less well-known is the fact that he also founded the Cavern Club in Liverpool, named after the Parisienne jazz club 'Le Caveau', where the Beatles made their name.

130. Barry Foster (1931-2002), known for his role as Van der Valk, was born in Beeston. Foster was a great friend of David Baron, better known as Harold Pinter, and appeared in several of his plays.

131. TV satirist John Bird, famous for That Was the Week That Was and more recently Bremner Bird and Fortune, was born in Nottingham in 1936.

Bird and Fortune

132. The actress Samantha Morton was born in Nottingham and spent her childhood in care. Samantha attended the West Bridgford Comprehensive School and the Central Junior Workshop. Her big break came when she was spotted by Woody Allen who gave her a part in 'Sweet and Lowdown' earning her an Oscar nomination. She starred in a number of high-profile films, such as 'Minority Report' and, closer to home, she's well known for her roles in TV series 'Cracker' and 'Band of Gold'. She also starred in the film 'Control', which was filmed in Nottingham.

133. Les Dawson lived on Gregory Boulevard before his comedy career was established. Later, he became a regular visitor to Nottingham when his daughter became a nurse at the Queen's Medical Centre.

134. Rock City has hosted many famous artists including David Bowie, U2, REM and Robbie Williams and also performers you might not expect like Dale Winton, Rolf Harris, Right Said Fred and PJ & Duncan.

135. The bean bags used in the Channel 4 reality series 'Big Bother' were manufactured by a Nottingham company called BeansBeans leading to a worldwide interest in such products.

136. Throughout the golden age of British cinema until the early 1970s, the majority of all cinema posters were printed by Stafford & Co. of Netherfield and Lonsdale & Bartholomew Ltd of Nottingham.

137. Legendary Soft Machine saxophonist Elton Dean was born in Nottingham.

138. Queen of Green, Penney Poyzer, star of 'No Waste Like Home', lives in West Bridgford in an eco-home with a showcase of green features, including worms in the toilet system.

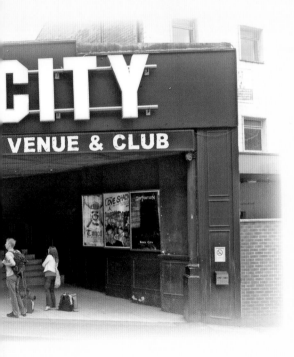

139. Ricky Gervais made his debut as a stand-up comedian in the mid-90s at the Just the Tonic comedy club, hosted by the Old Vic on Fletcher Gate.

140. Princess Margaret and Lord Snowden attended Nottingham Playhouse's gala opening night on December 11th 1963 to see Shakespeare's 'Coriolanus' featuring a young Ian McKellen and Leo McKern. The reception for the play ended in a punch-up at the Council House. If that wasn't enough excitement, the Beatles were also in town the day before appearing at the Odeon.

This theatre provided by the Nottingham Corporation for the presentation of plays was graced by the presence of The Earl of Snowdon on the opening night 11 December 1963

Nottingham Playhouse

141. The famous Selectadisc shops were founded by Hucknall lad Brian Selby, with outlets on Arkwright Street and other city centre locations. The sadly now defunct London branch features on the cover of the classic Oasis album 'What's the Story Morning Glory'. The Clash played an impromptu gig at the Nottingham Selectadisc Market Street branch in 1985.

142. Renowned Nottingham physician Dr Peter Toghill was asked to coach Dirk Bogarde in the finer points of 'rugger' when University College Hospital London was chosen as the film location for 'Doctor in the House'. It was also rumoured that Sir Lancelot Spratt, the larger-than-life character played by James Robertson Justice, was based on George Brownlee, a surgeon at Nottingham General Hospital where Toghill first worked in the 1950s.

143. Nottingham's Lady Bay bridge was once used as an Eastern Bloc rail crossing in the 1982 TV Series 'Smiley's People' based upon the novel by John le Carre that starred Sir Alec Guinness.

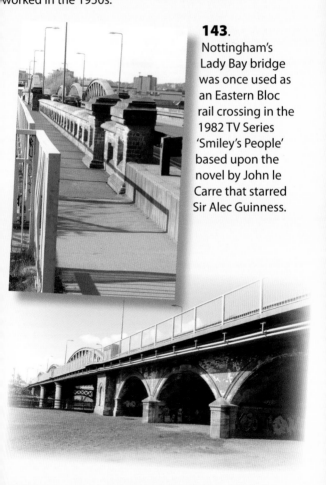

144. Veteran actor Michael Jayston was born in Nottingham on the 29th October 1935. He played Tsar Nicholas II in the Film 'Nicholas and Alexandra' and Quiller in the television series 'Quiller'. He was also considered for the part of James Bond, having played Bond in radio adaptations.

145. The cult film 'Withnail and I' is a personal favourite of designer Paul Smith. The character of Withnail was based on Vivian MacKerrell, an unusual chap who also hailed from Nottingham. He was a friend of Smith and studied at RADA. He helped out at the old Paul Smith warehouse packing boxes. Described by the film's writer Bruce Robinson as 'wild, aristocratic and highly educated', many of the character's exploits, like drinking lighter fuel, have more than a ring of truth. Apparently MacKerrell couldn't see for days after that particular experiment!

146. Mathew Horne, best known for his popular role in the hit comedy series 'Gavin and Stacey', 'Horne and Cordon' and various other sketch shows, was born in Nottingham. He lived in Burton Joyce and studied drama at Manchester University. Other little known facts about him are that he is an accomplished drummer and also supports Tottenham Hotspur.

147. Nottingham's first supergroup, Sons and Lovers, were the first group to appear in colour on BBC2 in a show called 'Colour Me Pop'. They performed every music show except Top of the Pops, but they never actually had a hit. Their most promising single 'Happiness in Love' never charted due to the record distributors being on summer holiday. The large advance orders for the single were never delivered.

148. Leslie Crowther (1933–1996) was from West Bridgford. His mother, Marie de Lisle, was Britain's first female stage manager.

149. Chris Gascoyne, best known as bigamist Peter Barlow in Coronation Street, was born in Sutton-in-Ashfield. He began his career at 16 as the bully Barry Kent in 'The Secret Diary of Adrian Mole'.

150. The world premiere of the film 'Sons and Lovers' took place in Nottingham at midnight on June 23rd 1960. Part of it was filmed around the local area, members of author D.H. Lawrence's family were in attendance.
More recently, both 'Pulp Fiction' and 'Silence of the Lambs' had their UK premieres at the Broadway Cinema in Nottingham.

151. Douglas Byng (1893-1987) the Mapperley-born entertainer, became one of the most celebrated pantomime dames billed as 'Bawdy but British' his songs were full of innuendo and double entendres. He made numerous recordings many of which were included on a collection entitled 'Naughty Nights with Douglas Byng'. Noel Coward once described his act as 'the most refined vulgarity in London'. His famous numbers included 'Sex Appeal Sarah', 'Milly the Messy Old Mermaid' and 'The Lass who Leaned against the Tower of Pisa'.

152. Micky Dolenz, star of 'Circus Boy' and drummer with the 1960's group 'The Monkees' lived at Winthorpe near Newark in the 1980s.

153. The 4th Duke of Portland became famous throughout England after creating the first sewage farm in the country at Flood Meadows in Clipstone. During the nineteenth century, the fifth Duke of Portland built a network of tunnels and rooms beneath his family seat at Welbeck Abbey – including a chapel, library and ballroom all lit by gas. It was alleged he suffered a painful shyness, and always kept his carriage windows covered when travelling.

154. Camille d'Hostun de la Baume, Duc de Tallard (1652–1728), captured at the Battle of Blenheim in 1704, was imprisoned in Newdigate House on Castle Gate. During his period of open imprisonment he was responsible for introducing both celery and bread rolls to the English public. There still exists a celery club at the house, which is home to the Nottingham and Nottinghamshire United Services Club.

155. Henry IV imprisoned Owen Glendower, son of the valiant Welsh chieftain of that name, in Nottingham Castle, while Scottish King David languished for eleven years in the castle's dungeons.

156. In September 1981 the Dovecote Inn in the village of Laxton was acquired by the Crown Estate, and remains the property of the Crown to this day.

Laxton farms are famous for a unique medieval three-field crop rotation system. The pub is one of only a handful of inns owned by the Royal Family.

Dovecote Inn (above)
Crown Estate sign (right)

157. Charles II gave a royal hunting lodge and land at Bestwood to his mistress Nell Gwyn – no doubt fo services rendered!
Bestwood Lodge was also very popular with Edward

158. The Prince of Wales, later King Edward VIII once

owned a farm in Lenton. In 1932 he told an Albert Hall audience 'I feel that I am somewhat of a citizen of this great city'. He purchased Grove Farm in 1927, ostensibly to house his herd of Pedigree shorthorns, but it became a pied-a-terre where he would take his lady friends.

It is also said that every time he visited Nottingham he required the Royal Train to stop at Radcliffe-on-Trent. Here he would visit his mistress Freda Dudley Ward of the Birkin family who lived at Lamcote House. He had an affair with her from 1918 for over ten years.

159. Richard III was resident in Nottingham in 1485 when he set off from Nottingham Castle to fight Henry Tudor, Earl of Richmond for the throne of England at Bosworth Field. Henry was victorious, being crowned Henry VII of England and beginning one of England's greatest royal lines.

160. King John died at Newark Castle in 1216 after seeing his treasures sink in the Wash.

l and Queen Alexandra, who were regular visitors. It as their use of the lodge that led to Daybrook railway ation being built on the Nottingham Suburban line.

161. Queen Eleanor of Castile, wife of Edward I, died at Harby in Nottinghamshire in November 1290. Her body was taken to Lincoln, embalmed and conveyed to London by a route marked with Eleanor crosses. Of the twelve crosses, only three originals have survived. Sadly, Edward said of his wife, "And I do not cease to love her now she is dead".

162. The 'Merrie Tales of the Mad Men of Gotam' are collected stories published in 1565 of Gotham's notorious local imbecilic population, but the imbeciles may have been a lot less mad than the tales would tell it. King John was considering building a new castle and thought the area might be suitable. At this time the local population had to fund the building of new castles, and the people of Gotham didn't particularly relish the prospect. Whenever the King or his men were in the vicinity, they pretended to be insane. The King was eventually put off. At the time it was thought that insanity was contagious.

In the 1880s, anglophile and regular visitor Washington Irving, author of Rip van Winkle, became taken with the tales. The antics therein reminding him very much of the people of New York. On returning home he gave New Yorkers the nickname 'Gothamites'.

Gotham City later became Batman's place of residence in the detective comics in 1941.

The Cuckoo Tale

The daft folk of Gotham heard a cuckoo calling from a bush. In an effort to prolong springtime, they built a fence around the bush to keep the bird in place. Of course, all their efforts were in vain when the cuckoo eventually flew away.

163. Franz Von Werra, a Second World War German POW escaped from prison camp and tried to leave the country in a Hurricane aircraft that wouldn't start because it was not fitted with a starter button.
He did eventually escape after being transferred to Canada, via an arduous route that included South America. His exploits are recorded in the 1957 film 'The One That Got Away', starring Hardy Kruger.

164. The Nags Head on Mansfield Road was once the hostelry where condemned men were offered a last drink on their final journey from the town prisons to the gallows, when they were sited on the junction of Mansfield Road and Forest Road. Legend has it that one condemned man refused a drink and so missed a reprieve that arrived minutes after his execution. Perhaps unsurprisingly, the pub is now reputed to be one of the most haunted buildings in the city.

165. St. Ann's Well, known variously since the 13ᵗʰ century as 'Owswell' and 'Robynhode Well', was once believed to possess healing powers. Supposedly able to restore virility, it was a regular attraction for day trips; even James I is said to have sampled the waters when visiting the area. The well vanished under a railway embankment around 100 years ago, but was recently rediscovered at the back of the Gardeners Pub.

166. Nestled in the parkland of Stapleford Hill sits a striking geological oddity, the Hemlock Stone. Referred to in D.H. Lawrence's 'Sons and Lovers' as a 'gnarled twisted lump of rock', it has been subject to an endless number of theories and outlandish myths. One has it that one night a sleepless monk in the Lenton Priory felt the presence of the devil and prayed to God, which woke the devil who angrily threw a mass of rock. The rock missed and came to rest on the side of Stapleford Hill. A somewhat more plausible, if a little less fun, explanation suggests that the sandstone outcrop is resistant to weathering due to an irregular compositional cementing of barium sulphate forming a cap.

167. It's widely known that Robin Hood once lived in Sherwood Forest, in a village known as Barnsdale. But less widely known is that at one time, Sherwood Forest extended to within a few miles of the current city centre, and some historians believe that Barnsdale was situated where Old Basford is today.

168. The Major Oak is estimated to be 800 to 1,000 years old. It weighs a massive 23 tons, has a girth of 33 feet and its branches span 92 feet. In 2001 it was voted England's Best Loved Tree, though competition probably wasn't fierce. It has now been cloned and it is possible to buy one.

169. The Thrust Measuring Rig, better known as 'The Flying Bedstead', a prototype vertical take off aircraft and the forerunner to the Harrier Jump Jet, was tested at Hucknall by Rolls Royce in 1954.

The Heyworth brothers, Harvey and Jim, completed more than 400 hours of testing on the Flying Bedstead. They spent many years living in Papplewick, and were also pioneers in the development of the jet engine. In December 1948 Harvey became the first man in the world to complete 1,000 hours flying time in a jet aircraft. He also famously landed a Lancaster on Hollinwell golf course during a ladies' golf match.

170. Ibuprofen was discovered in Nottingham. Early work on the project took place in a terraced house in Lady Bay between1953 and 1960. By 1983 it had become the fourth most popular prescription drug in the USA, as well as the first prescription drug to move to non-prescription status in the UK, when it became available over the counter in the same year. The team won the Queen's Award for Technology in 1985.

171. HP Sauce was invented by grocer Frederick Gibson Garton of Basford and originally made in Sandon St, New Basford. Garton offered many spicy products that found a ready market among the changing palates of British families returning from the colonies.

The name was registered in 1896 after Garton heard it was available in a restaurant in the Houses of Parliament. He later sold the recipe and brand for £150 to Edwin Samson Moore of the Midland Vinegar Company to pay a debt.

172. James Samuel Archer (1854–1920) co-invented the famous Sturmey Archer three-speed bicycle gears. He worked for the Raleigh Cycle Company and lived in Notttingham.

173. The Spinning Jenny was invented by James Hargreaves, who left Lancashire when his new invention was wrecked by rivals. He settled in Nottingham and built a small spinning mill just off Lower Parliament Street. It led to massive changes in the textile industry.

Richard Arkwright set up two of the world's first cotton mills in Nottingham in 1768. Twenty years later there were 28 cotton mills in the county, but few survived due to a lack of fast-flowing streams. The building which housed Hockley Mill still survives today.

174. One of the first-ever videotape recorders – the Telecan – was invented in Carlton in the early 1960s by Norman Rutherford and Michael Turner (Rutherford was an electrical engineer who ran a business repairing televisions). It was an expensive luxury item, and was actually mounted to the television cabinet. A model was displayed in the Nottingham Industrial Museum at Wollaton Hall before it closed in 2010.

175. John Peake Knight was a railwayman from Nottingham who designed signalling systems. He saw the potential of adapting these ideas for the ever-expanding transport systems. He is also credited with being one of the first to introduce the emergency communication cord on trains.

His main idea was a traffic control system for busy roads. The original invention was a semaphore signal with alternating red and green lights powered by gas which could be seen by day and night. It took several years before the plan was implemented but on December 9th 1868 the world's first traffic lights were introduced in London at the junction of Great George St. and Bridge St. near Westminster Bridge.

It was an immediate success but within a month

disaster struck. Leaky gas connections led to one of the traffic lights exploding injuring the policeman who was operating the signals. The lights continued functioning until 1872 but were not replaced. It wasn't until 1929 that traffic lights were introduced again in London.

176. In 1730 a stockinger named Draper of Bellar Gate, Nottingham produced the first pair of cotton stockings in England. By the end of the 18th century Nottingham was producing a third of all English stockings.

177. Calverton clergyman William Lee is credited with the invention of the first knitting machine in 1589. It is said that he did so because a lady with whom he was enamoured spent too much time knitting and not enough with him. A true romantic! Sadly, fears that the machine would cause mass unemployment forced him to take his invention to France where he died in poverty.

178. In 1813, Nottingham framesmith John Leavers (1786-1848) invented a machine capable of incorporating intricate patterns into lace, so beginning Nottingham's association as the lace capital of the world. You can see a plaque commemorating him on the Canning Circus island in Nottingham Derby Road.

179. In 1786 George Robinson and Sons of Papplewick became the first textile business to use steam-powered looms. After a disagreement with the fifth Lord Byron (great-uncle of the poet) the river Leen was dammed at Newstead, cutting off the water supply to the mills. Necessity became the mother of invention though, and rotary steam engines were installed to circumvent the move.

180. In the 1990's Professor Don Grierson of the University of Nottingham headed the team that produced the first genetically-engineered tomato. A puree made from the tomato was the first genetically modified food to be sold in the UK.

181. The Magnetic Resonance Imaging (MRI) Scanner was invented by Sir Peter Mansfield in the Physics

Department of the University of Nottingham in the early 1970s. He was fascinated by Hitler's V1 and V2 rockets during the Second World War, and at the age of 17, he joined the rocket propulsion department at the Ministry of Supply. His revolutionary work on MRI earned him the Nobel Prize for Medicine in 2003.

182. Nottingham-born physicist Louis Essen (1908–1997) built the first accurate atomic clock in 1955. It was accurate to one second in 300 years! During his lifetime Essen was also instrumental in advancements of radar technology, measurement of the speed of light and even published work that challenged Einstein's theory of relativity.

183. G.H. Hurt & Son Ltd, founded in 1912, were producers of cashmere and luxurious lace shawls which were worn by many famous Hollywood starlets such as Vivien Leigh in 'Gone With the Wind' and Julie Christie in 'Dr Zhivago'. More recently they were worn by the cast in 'Bleak House' and 'Pride and Prejudice'.

G.H. Hurt & Son premises

184. George Brough (1890-1970) produced the Brough Superior motorcycle on Haydn Road, Sherwood between 1919 and 1935, and Vernon Road, Basford between 1935 and 1940. An entirely hand-built machine, it was described as 'the Rolls Royce of motorcycles' by The Motor Cycle magazine. Brough lived locally at Pendine in Redhill, named after Pendine Sands where he set many motorcycle speed records.

Brough also produced a high quality car, the Dual Purpose. The war brought an end to production, and only around 3,000 motorcycles and 100 cars were ever built.

Brough Superior 1000cc 'Old Bill' 1922

"51 firsts in a row and then the backside torn out of my trousers."

This was company owner George Brough's account of a remarkable run of success on 'Old Bill', his personal racing motorcycle.

The run of victories came to an abrupt end in 1923 with Brough crashing at Clipstone Circuit near Mansfield.

The motorcycle was named 'Old Bill' after a popular First World War cartoon character.

Restored by Roger Allen and kindly leaned to the Museum by Mrs. Sue Allen.

Brough's most-famous patron was T.E. Lawrence (Lawrence of Arabia), who fell in love with the motorcycle's speed and craftsmanship. He eloquently described the experience as "the motorcycle with a touch of blood in it" and as "better than all the riding animals on earth".

On returning from the desert, Lawrence served in the RAF under the assumed name of Ross. While serving at RAF Cranwell he paid three shillings a day to Ruby Briant of Newark. Though no proof of a romantic link exists, neither does any explanation for the payments. Lawrence owned seven Brough Superiors, and died in circumstances which remain somewhat mysterious, riding a Brough Superior SS100.

Pendine House where Brough lived for many years

185. Gordon Fogg (1919–2005) was a Langar-born botanist whose work led to the understanding of photosynthesis and nitrogen fixation. During the Second World War his work led to the development of water-soluble parachutes, which enabled the Allies to drop mines at sea. He was awarded the CBE in 1985 for his contribution to science.

186. Silicones were discovered by Frederick Kipping (1863–1949) in 1904 at University College, Nottingham, then in Shakespeare Street in the building now occupied by Nottingham Trent University. His work led to the development of the global synthetic rubber and silicone-based lubricant industries.

187. Brandy-snaps were first made commercially by Sharp and Nickless of 72 College Street, Long Eaton. From as far back as 1888 the Nottinghamshire company was exporting them as far away as Australia.

They were probably first invented by the medieval French or Belgians, who called them 'gaufrettes'.

188. During the 1960's, Nottingham company S. Thomas and Co. of Bulwell were regarded as the largest manufacturers of drinking straws in the world. Unfortunately, the introduction of cheap imports and changes of can sizes led to a decline in their usage and the eventual closure of the factory in 1983.

189. During World War Two, one of the first production units for the manufacture of penicillin (by the bottle culture method) and the largest in the UK was built in Daleside Road, Nottingham by the Ministry of Supply and managed by Boots. The penicillin mould was grown in huge quantities of quart milk bottles. The building still stands today.

190. In 1901, Edgar Hooley, Nottingham's County Surveyor, developed tarmac and obtained a British Patent a year later. Radcliffe Road in Nottingham became the first tarmac laid road in the world.

191. Augusta Ada King, 1815–1852, Countess of Lovelace and daughter of Lord Byron, the famous poet, is recognised as the world's first computer programmer. She wrote a plan that could calculate Bernoulli numbers that was used on Babbage's Analytical Engine (1989–91). She died at age 32, the same age as her father died and of the same cause to boot: namely, medicinal bloodletting. She's buried at Hucknall next to Lord Byron.
On December 10th 1980, the anniversary of Ada's birthday, the US Defense Department approved its new reference manual for computer programming which it called ADA. Her image can be seen in the Microsoft product authenticity hologram stickers.

192. In 1900, the Nottingham suburb of Basford had the biggest concentration of wicker furniture and pram manufacturers in the UK with several factories employing hundreds of workers. Basford and other centres such as Colwick and Toton had over 400 acres under willow cultivation. William Scaling of Basford was, in Queen Victoria's reign, willow grower by Royal Appointment and stated that the best and finest willows in the United Kingdom came from Nottingham. He helped patent a device for splitting willow and was instrumental in the manufacture of willow furniture and prams.

193. In 1832 Herbert Ingram (1811-1860) established his own printing and newsagent's business in Nottingham. He noticed that when newspapers included woodcut illustrations their sales increased. He deduced that it would be possible to make good profits from an illustrated newspaper.
His newsagent business however failed to make much progress until, totally unrelated, he purchased the rights to a laxative known as 'Parrs Life Pills'. The profits from selling these pills provided the funds which enabled him to set up and publish the 'Illustrated London News' in 1842.

194. The Bramley apple began its life around 1809 when Mary Ann Brailsford of Southwell enjoyed an apple so much she planted the pips. One germinated, and when Matthew Bramley bought the house in 1846 the tree was producing a good crop of apples. Today, over 100,000 tonnes of Bramley apples, worth £50m, are sold every year – all originating from the same tree which still stands in Southwell.

Above: Bramley Tree Cottage, Southwell
Centre: The Bramley apple tree at the rear of the cottage
Below: A plaque erected at the base of the tree

THE TREE COUNCIL
IN CELEBRATION OF
THE GOLDEN JUBILEE OF
HER MAJESTY
QUEEN ELIZABETH II
has designated
THE ORIGINAL BRAMLEY
one of fifty
GREAT BRITISH TREES
in recognition of its place
in the national heritage
JUNE 2002
Supported by National Grid

National Grid

195. One of the most remarkable physicists of the 19th century was miller and self-taught mathematician George Green (1793–1841) of Sneinton, whose 1827 essay on electricity and magnetism has been described as the beginning of mathematical physics in England. On his historic visit to Nottingham in 1930, Einstein paid him homage. Green's mathematical techniques are still regularly employed in nuclear and solid-state physics today. He is buried in St. Stephen's Churchyard, Sneinton.

Green's Mill at Sneinton

196. In 1930, Albert Einstein visited the fledgling University College, Nottingham to lecture on the theory of relativity. His board writings, as well as the chalk he used, are retained by the University to this day.

197. In October 1931, Mahatma Ghandhi visited Beeston to call on his nephew, J.V. Joshi, who was lodging in Linden Grove, Beeston and studying at University College, Nottingham.

198. Dame Stella Rimington, who became Director General of M15 in 1991, lived in Nottingham and attended the Nottingham Girl's High School. After joining the British High Commission in India, where she worked as a secretary, she rose to prominence and went on to work in all the main fields of the security service, including counter subversion, counter espionage and counter terrorism.

199. Thomas Helwys, who built the first Baptist church on English soil at Spitalfields, London in 1611, was born in Nottingham and raised on the Broxtowe Hall estate.

200. Thomas Cranmer was born in Aslockton in the parish of Whatton in 1489. In 1532 he became the first Protestant Archbishop of Canterbury and is regarded as the founder of the Church of England.

201. The famous, or rather the infamous, Charlie Peace (1832-1879) was a frequenter of Nottingham's alehouses. At the lower end of Pilcher Gate, at its junction with Fletcher Gate, stands an old public-house called 'The Windmill'. Here from his resting place now called 'Charlie's Corner' he would plot his robberies. His life has been romanticised in many films and novels including a Sherlock Homes story 'The Adventure of The Illustrious Client'.

Charlie Peace on the fiddle

202. Polish Prime Minister General Wladyslaw Sikorski (1881–1943) perished in a suspicious aeroplane crash in Gibraltar during the Second World War while leading the Polish government in exile. The entire incident is shrouded in mystery, but don't hold your breath, the official file is to remain secret until 100 years after his death. He was buried in Newark, in the Polish cemetery, to be returned to his home country only when 'Poland was free'. He was reinterred in Poland in 1993.

203. Songwriter and musician Edwin Starr, who enjoyed many chart successes, including his song 'War' (later covered by artists as diverse as Frankie Goes to Hollywood and Bruce Springsteen), died in Beeston in 2003 and is buried in Wilford Hill Cemetery. His very last interview was conducted by Queen's Medical Centre hospital radio.

204. The inspiration for Jamie Oliver's campaign for healthy school dinners was Jeanette Orrey, dinner lady at St. Peter's Primary School in East Bridgford. Jamie visited the school a number of times between 2002 and 2003.

205. Nottingham can lay claim to its very own Dalek. Nicholas Pegg, a former pupil at Nottingham High School, played a Dalek in the Christopher Ecclestone series of 'Dr Who'. He is also the author of the reference book 'The Complete David Bowie' as well as a pantomime script writer.

206. In 1799, seven-year-old Robert Blincoe was sold to work in the Gonalston Mill in Lowdham. In 1822, journalist John Brown interviewed Blincoe for an article about child labour, and decided to write his biography. Australian academic John Waller believes there is strong evidence that Charles Dickens read these memoirs and based Oliver Twist fiction's most famous orphan on Blincoe's early life.

SIR BARNES NEVILLE WALLIS

1897 - 1979

SLEPT HERE DURING W.W.II

207. During the Second World War, Barnes Wallis, inventor of the Bouncing Bomb, lodged at the Middleton Inn (now the Dewdrop Inn) on the outskirts of Ilkeston. Some also believe that Guy Gibson, who led the Dambusters raid, lived for a time in East Bridgford.

208. Before he became leader of the Labour Party, Hugh Gaitskell lectured in economics for the Workers' Educational Association to miners in Nottinghamshire where he also made his first political speech.

209. John Player began his tobacco business as a sideline, but quickly gained an edge over his competitors with low prices and intelligent marketing. His tobacco came in ready-rolled cigarettes packaged with his name and a sketch of Nottingham Castle.

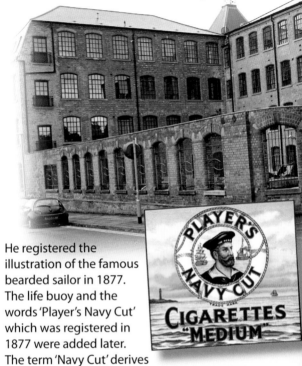

He registered the illustration of the famous bearded sailor in 1877. The life buoy and the words 'Player's Navy Cut' which was registered in 1877 were added later. The term 'Navy Cut' derives from the old custom of squeezing a plug of tobacco in a piece of canvas and cutting off a slice when required.

210. Sir Hugh Willoughby, a descendant of the original owner of Wollaton Hall, was a famous Elizabethan explorer who perished in the Arctic in 1554 on an expedition to discover a north-east passage to Cathay and India.

211. George Vason, was born in North Muskham near Newark. In 1797 he went to Tonga as a missionary. He quickly 'went native' and became the first white man to be made a South Sea Island chief. He came back to Nottingham and became Governor of Nottingham Gaol.

The old Raleigh factory on Raleigh Street

212. Jesse Boot picked up his knowledge of the curative properties of plants while helping his agricultural labourer father in the fields. He'd then study pharmacy late into the night.

A pioneer in retailing who saw the merit in buying in bulk and selling cheaply, he became so successful his competitors thought he was selling adulterated drugs. His answer was to rename his business The Boots Pure Drug Company. The most popular product Jesse Boot ever produced was the 'Boots No Name Ointment'.

213. In 1886 Frank Bowden was sent home from the Far East expecting to live only a few months. His doctor advised him to take up the new fad of cycling. After recovering his health he tracked down a small bike supplier on Raleigh Street, bought the company and turned it into the world's largest bike factory.

214. Stars who have attended events at Broadway Cinema include Quentin Tarantino and Charlton Heston. Tarantino visited the 'Shots in the Dark' murder mystery festivals where he showed the world's first rough cut version of 'Pulp Fiction' to a packed audience.

Quentin Tarantino poster signed complete with spelling mistake

215. The Humber automobile marque began its life as Thomas Humber's bicycle company in Beeston in 1868. From 1880-1907 Humber Road was the main factory for making bicycles and cars. After 1907 car manufacturing moved to Coventry.

Remains of the Humber factory

216. Colonel John Hutchinson, close ally of Cromwell and the Governor of Nottingham Castle was the 13th of 39 Commissioners to sign the death warrant of King Charles I. He spent several thousand pounds purchasing the art treasures of the late king following his execution. Among the works was Titian's masterpiece 'Venus and the Organ Player'. which now hangs in the Gemaldegalerie in Berlin and 'Pardo Venus' which now hangs in the Louvre. From the palaces of Whitehall and Madrid, 'Venus and the Organ Player' once found its way to Hutchinson's humble Nottinghamshire estate.

217. Beeston-born Paul Smith, founder of the eponymous fashion brand, was training to be a professional racing cyclist when a bad accident hospitalised him. On discharge he began to frequent The Bell public house with friends he made in hospital. The venue was a magnet for designers and art students.

218. Professor Angus Wallace is regarded as being one of Nottingham's most famous surgeons and is credited with many innovations. He hit the headlines in 1995 when he performed emergency surgery on a passenger who had suffered a collapsed lung while travelling on a jumbo jet to Hong Kong. The make-shift operation involved using a coat hanger sterilised in brandy and mineral water.

219. There is a plaque in the Park Estate where Rt. Hon. W. E. Gladstone felled a tree on May 11th 1875.

One of his hobbies was chopping down trees just for fun, and occasionally to impress the ladies. Gladstone, who was four times prime minister, was once the MP for Newark. He was a friend of the Duke of Newcastle and a trustee of the Park Estate.

220. Edmund Allenby (1861–1936), 1st Viscount and Field Marshal was responsible for a brilliant victory over the Turks at Megiddo and for liberating Jerusalem during the First World War. He was born at Brackenhurst near Southwell where there is a commemorative plaque.

221. Ruddington-born Caleb Wood, Robert Tongue and James Marshall were heroic defenders of Rorke's Drift, where in 1879, 139 British soldiers successfully fended off an attack by over 4,000 Zulu warriors. All three men were buried in Ruddington cemetery. Their commander, Lieutenant Gonville Bromhead, was from Newark.

222. The UK's first children's library was founded in Nottingham in 1882 by Samuel Morley.

223. Nottingham was the first place in England to record an earthquake in 1180.

224. The world's first school for adults was set up in Nottingham in 1798.

225. In 1863, Nottingham's Victoria Street was the location of the first subway for conducting sewers and gas pipes outside of London. Lighting was added in 1875.

226. The first regional branch of the National Film Theatre opened in Nottingham in 1966.

227. Nottingham was the first city to install Braille signs in its shopping centres.

228. The first aerial press photograph was taken in Nottingham in 1910.

229. In July 1840, members of the Mechanics Institution enjoyed the world's first railway excursion to the Leicester Institution.

230. Nottingham High Street is one of the shortest high streets of a major UK city.

231. A small shop in Nottingham opened the first Urdu library in the UK in 1967.

232. Richard Sankey took advantage of the Permian Marls at Bulwell, Nottingham, to start his own company in 1855. Sankey's products were to become an essential part of the Victorian garden scene. As early as 1912, the firm was making an incredible 500,000 flower pots a week ; the largest pots weighed nearly a hundredweight each, with an ingenious false bottom to facilitate removal of the plant without disturbing the roots.

The pottery was so productive it had its own railway sidings and even in those early days Sankey products were exported all over the world.

233. Nottingham set up the first police forensic laboratory in 1934, headed by Professor Holden, a botanist from University College. Nottingham police also sent the first radio message by police car in 1932. It was claimed these two innovations cut crime by 13.5% during their first year of joint operation. They were both introduced by the somewhat controversial Chief Constable Athelstan Popkess, a South African army officer, who had been appointed despite having no UK policing experience.

234. High pressure water supply was first developed and operated in Nottingham in 1831 by the Trent Waterways Company at Trent Bridge, under the supervision of 25 year-old company engineer Thomas Hawksley (1807-1893). He was born in Arnold, a suburb of Nottingham.

235. In 1962, Nottingham's Eric Irons, who lived in Top Valley, became Britain's first black magistrate. During his lifetime he championed a number of local and national causes for equality and social justice, and was named Nottingham's Citizen of Honour in 1996.

236. The first-ever organic sugar beet crop was grown in Newark in 2001.

237. Nottingham was the first city in the country to have a Half-day Closing Association.

238. Vacuum cleaner expert James Brown, known as 'Mr Vacuum Cleaner', opened the first museum dedicated entirely to vacuum cleaners on Nottingham Road in Eastwood.

239. Smith's Bank, founded in Nottingham in 1658 by draper and Father of English banking Thomas Smith, was the first provincial bank in England, and the first to open a branch in London. It predates the Bank of England by six years and any bank outside London by 92 years. It was also the first private bank in the country to issue paper money.

Nottingham Smiths Bank Branch
The Oldest Provincial
Bank in England

In 1658 Thomas Smith (1631 - 1699) completed the purchase for £210 of premises near to this site, where he commenced trade as a Mercer and where the family banking business developed shortly thereafter.

Abel Smith II (1717 - 1788) founded further Smiths Banks in London 1758, Lincoln 1775 and Hull 1784. A bank at Derby was established in 1806.

These Smiths family banks were organised as partnerships until 1902 when they amalgamated with the Union Bank of London. Subsequent mergers with National Provincial Bank of England in 1918 and the Westminster Bank in 1968 created the present National Westminster Bank PLC.

Smiths family motto - Fidelity, with industry and with honour.

240. The world's heaviest trifle was made at Clarendon College in 1990, weighing in at a whopping 3.13 tons.

241. On May 11th 2005 in Rempstone, Peter Dowerswell gobbled his way into the record books by swallowing 24 sausages in 45 seconds – smashing the previous record of 15 sausages in 60 seconds, and only stopping short of more because his supply ran out.

242. Founded in 1296, Goose Fair is the oldest fair of any kind in the world.

243. With only 22 seats, the Screen Room, now called Screen 22, on Nottingham's Broad Street claims to be the smallest cinema in the world. Early booking is advisable.

244. Agatha Christie's 'The Mousetrap', which holds the record for the world's longest-running play, started life on October 6th 1952 at the Theatre Royal Nottingham with Richard Attenborough as Detective Sergeant Trotter. Nottingham was chosen for the premiere as it was regarded a 'lucky' city for Agatha Christie's shows. 'The Hollow', 'Witness for the Prosecution' and 'Spider's Web' all premiered in Nottingham.

245. Nottingham University was the first UK university to establish a campus in China at Ningbo.

246. In 1918, eight tons of TNT exploded at the National Shell Filling Factory in Chilwell. 134 people were killed, of whom only 32 could be positively identified. The blast was allegedly heard up to 20 miles away.

247. American owners GEM opened Britain's first major out-of-town supermarket in West Bridgford in 1964. One further store was opened in Leeds in the following year, before the controlling interest was acquired by ASDA.

248. The first STD call, or call without the aid of an operator, was made in Nottingham by Alderman J. Llewellyn from the Nottingham Council House on January 3rd 1962. The receiver of the call was Herbert Ireland in Belfast.

249. The village of Wellow is the site of the tallest permanent maypole in the UK. The maypole, recently replaced, stands over 55 feet tall.

250. The garden allotments in St. Ann's, which date back to 1830, are both the oldest and largest allotments in the UK. It was known as the Hungerhills area when it was first mentioned in 1604/5. The 75 acre site has been grade 2 listed.

251. The sailors who fought at Trafalgar wore shrink-proof, double-lap worsted jackets which were made on Nottingham warp frames.

252. In 1972, Fred Ellis baked the world's biggest pork pie weighing a belly-busting 60lb 6oz. Known as the King of the Pie Men, Fred made pies for celebrities like Danny La Rue, Bob Hope and he even made a football-shaped pie for Brian Clough.

253. The 'open doors' principle employed by psychiatric hospitals, whereby patients are allowed to move freely from room to room, was pioneered at Mapperley Hospital in 1952.

254. Nottingham Prison was the first prison workshop to install injection-moulding machinery so that the inmates could make plimsolls and slippers!

255. Notts-born flyer Vincent Arrowsmith was one of three crewmen of 139 Squadron who took off in a Bristol Blenheim on the first British bombing mission of the Second World War, just 45 minutes after Prime Minister Neville Chamberlain declared war on Germany on September 3rd 1939.

256. At 5.5 acres, Nottingham boasts the biggest market square in England and in Car Colston, Nottinghamshire can boast the largest village green in Europe.

Car Colston village green

257. Peter Glazebrook of Halam, near Southwell, has held eight world records for growing giant vegetables. In September 2010 he held two world records, one for the heaviest parsnip and the world record for the longest beetroot.

258. Nottingham Forest were the first football club to spend £1 million on a player when they signed Trevor Francis in 1979. The exact fee before taxes was actually £999,999 – as Brian Clough was concerned the record might go to the player's head.

'There's only room for one big head in this club young man.'

259. At Coxmore Golf Club, nine-year-old Rhiannon Linacre of Kirkby-in-Ashfield went into the record books in 2006 when she became the youngest female golfer to score a hole in one. She actually thought she'd lost the ball before she found it in the hole!

260. The UK's first radio phone-in was on Radio Nottingham on 4th February 1968. It is believed the topic was about the use of pest control.

261. At 10.5 tonnes, Little John, the largest bell in the Council House, has the deepest tone of any bell in the UK. As a result, its sound travels further than any other bell in the country – up to seven miles on a clear day.

262. Carburton and Perlethorpe's parish registers date back to 1528, making them some of the oldest in England.

263. In 1994, local boy Jim Lees (1912–2001) was nominated for the Guinness Book of Records as the world's longest-serving Scout with 73 years in the movement.

264. Air ace Johnnie Johnson (1915–2001), who studied at University College, Nottingham, holds the record for most kills during the Second World War. His application to the Auxiliary Air Force was actually turned down, and he was only accepted for the RAF Volunteer Reserve.

265. Henry 'Harry' Cursham, the Wilford-born centre forward who played for Notts County in the 19th century, still holds the FA Cup all-time goalscoring record with an amazing 48 goals (four more than Ian Rush), including 6 in an 11-1 victory over Wednesday Strollers in 1882.

266. In 1955, at the Portland Cinema in Sutton-in-Ashfield, 'Syncopating Sandy' Strickland set the world record for non-stop piano playing with a staggering 133 hours and 14 minutes, beating his own record set only months previously in Newark.

267. In 1936 Barton Buses ran what is believed to be the first continental tour by a British coach company. 270 guests travelled via Dover to Brussels, Cologne and various German cities for the princely sum of 23 guineas. This inventive company was the first to use female conductors, and also the first to introduce diesel-driven buses as far back as 1930.

T.H. BARTON
OBE
(THE GUV'NOR)
1866-1946
Engineer, inventor, innovator
Pioneer of motor bus transport

Worked here
1913-1946

268. In the east of Nottinghamshire near Eakring lies a band of rock known as Sherwood (or Nottingham Castle) sandstone, which holds Nottingham's oilfield. It was the first commercial oilfield in the UK sector (predating the North Sea by 21 years) with production beginning in 1943. The field contributed 2,269,305 barrels of oil to the war effort, which is equivalent to about 43 fully-laden tankers. The oil was actually of a higher grade than that found in the Middle East or the North Sea. Eakring last produced oil in 1989 but tests have been carried out since to determine whether there are sufficient reserves to justify new drilling operations.

Sir Frank Whittle invented a jet-powered drill, which was developed at Eakring and Kirklington Hall and used for the first time at Plungar, a few miles from Eakring. Other oil-drilling techniques, such as slant drilling, were also first developed and tested at Eakring.

Nodding donkey Eakring

The Eakring memorial
'Americans working in cooperation with British
drilling effort 1943'

269.The finest rockery stone is Bulwell stone, which hardens under water and germinates moss much earlier than other stone. It's been popular among royal gardeners for several generations!

270. Mapperley Plains is a layer of very hard impervious rock which has suffered little erosion. It is said that if you travelled due east from Dorket Head, the next time you would reach land of similar height would be at the Ural Mountains in Russia. The grand structure of St. Pancras Station was built with bricks from the Mapperley Brickworks.

271. The poor and porous soils in the north of Nottighamshire cannot retain water, leading to a natural cover of Oak Birch and bracken. This is what gave rise to Sherwood Forest, where the legend of Robin Hood was born. The soils to the south of the county are based on the Mercia Mudstone, giving a rich pasture which supports dairying – and this has given rise to the famous Colston Bassett Stilton cheese.

272. The headquarters of the British Geological Survey founded in 1835, and the world's oldest national geological survey, are in Keyworth.

273.Originally known as Tiggua Cobaucc, meaning 'Place of Caves', Nottingham has more man-made caves than anywhere else in Britain. Some of the caves date back to medieval times.

The caves beneath Nottingham Castle

274. The Luddites were formed in 1811 in Nottingham under Gravener Henson (or Ned Ludlam – better known as Ned Ludd), allegedly a self-educated ex-stockinger from Bulwell. The first Luddite activity occurred in Arnold on March 11th 1811 when 60 stocking frames were broken in protest at changes brought about during the Industrial Revolution, and more frames were later destroyed by a mob in Bulwell.

275. Colonel Francis Hacker of East Bridgford was one of the regicides of King Charles I, and was later tried and executed at Tyburn for treason. Despite his plea that he was only following orders, General Henry Ireton of Attenborough was one of the signatories to Charles' death warrant. In 1660, Charles II requested Ireton's corpse, along with that of Oliver Cromwell, to be exhumed and mutilated in retribution.

276. Jeremiah Brandreth, the Nottingham Captain of the 1817 Pentrich Rebellion, was born in Wilford and later moved to Sutton-in-Ashfield. He was tried and executed for high treason, and along with two of his co-conspirators was one of the last men to be sentenced to be hanged, drawn and quartered in Britain.

277. Thrumpton Hall was the family seat of the Powdrills for five centuries before they were dispossessed of it for their complicity in the Gunpowder Plot in 1605.

Thrumpton Hall

278. The Union of Democratic Mineworkers was set up after Roy Lynk and a group of Nottinghamshire miners refused to strike during the 1984 National Union of Mineworkers' strikes, on the basis that no national ballot on strike action had taken place. The decision led to a bitter division among miners and the eventual break-up of the NUM.

279. Detective Chief Superintendent Leonard 'Nipper' Read, famous for bringing the Kray twins to justice, solving the 'Babes in the Wood' murders and investigating 'The Great Train Robbery' was born in Bobbers Mill, Nottingham in 1925. Nipper was too small for the Nottingham force so therefore he joined the London Metropolitan Police Force in 1947 as they had a lower height requirement. Coincidentally both Kray twins spent their last days in Nottinghamshire prisons (Reggie in Nottingham Prison and Ronnie at Rampton).

280. Lady Mary Wortley Montagu was born in 1689 at Thoresby Hall in Nottinghamshire. She lead a very colourful life, which included membership of the Hell Fire Club in London. She is best known for bringing the practice of smallpox inoculation to England, following a trip to the Ottoman Empire. Her brother had earlier died from smallpox and she had been badly scarred by the disease. She encountered a great deal of prejudice at what was then a rather radical idea, and it was not until Jenner developed the safer practice of vaccination with the cowpox vaccine, that inroads were made into defeating the disease. She died in 1762.

Thoresby Hall

281. In 1981, Notts County FC released a song called 'County's the Team for Me' to celebrate promotion to the old first division. It gained national infamy when Radio One DJ Noel Edmonds labelled it the worst pop record of all time. Sadly it didn't stop the team from running out onto the pitch to the song until 2004.

282. King Charles I was sold to Parliament for the then-equivalent value of £400,000 after surrendering to the Scottish army at the Saracen's Head, Southwell in May 1647. The pub was called the King's Head at the time, and it is ironic that the King lost his own head as a consequence of his actions. Oliver Cromwell also spent a night or two there not long after.

283. Low Marnham boasts several memorials to its talented and eccentric sons, the Cartwright brothers. Ingenious clergyman Edmund invented the power loom in 1784. 'Father of Reform' John was a parliamentary reformer and radical, publishing a document that became the basis for Chartist reform some 60 years later. Explorer George 'Labrador' Cartwright wrote the first sociological study of the Eskimos. He even brought five back with him to England to be received by King George III.

284. Built in the early 70s in Bulwell Nottingham, Lunar Estate is Britain's only housing estate to be named after astronauts involved in the Apollo moon landings.

285. In 1734, the Mayor of Nottingham was bowled over with a 100lb cheese during a riot after stall-holders at an annual market had increased cheese prices by more than a third.

The Battle of Nottingham

286. John Deane (1678-1761) Nottingham's best known pirate led an eventful life. He helped the Royal Navy to capture Gibraltar from the Spanish in 1704. Now a Captain, John Dean left the navy and bought his own ship the 'Nottingham Galley'. Wrecked off the coast of New England on a small rock called Boon Island, the crew had to resort to cannibalism to survive. John Deane joined the Russian Navy in 1714 to help Peter The Great in the war with Sweden. His raids on Swedish ships earned him the reputation as a pirate. He was eventually court martialled for losing two prize ships and served a year's detention.

Dean returned to England and worked in the consular service as a diplomat and spy. He retired in Wilford village with his wife Sarah and died August the 18th 1761. Sarah died the day before.

287. In 1852, The
Great Northern Railway
and The Midland Railway were in
dispute over the rights to run services.
The matter came to a head when employees
and officials of the Midland Railway decided to
hijack a Great Northern engine. The hapless engine was
surrounded by Midland locomotives, shunted into an
old shed and held captive. The lines were then pulled
up to prevent escape.
It took seven months before tensions between the two
railway companies were resolved and the captured
train was eventually released.

THE GOOD, THE BRAVE AND THE QUIRKY

288. Between 1945 and 1965, local farrier George Flinders built a tower from used horseshoes in Scarrington, near Newark. Today it contains 50,000 horseshoes and stands an impressive 17 feet tall!

289. The Pauncefoot Family, former owners of Stoke Hall, were descendants of Abel Smith the Nottingham banker. Sir Julian Pauncefote (1828–1902) was the first British ambassador to the United States and is buried in East Stoke churchyard.

290. Slawomir Rawicz (1915–2004) was a Polish officer captured by the Russians in 1939 and exiled to Siberia. He claimed to have escaped with six others and walked some 4,000 miles south through the Gobi Desert and over the Himalayas to India.

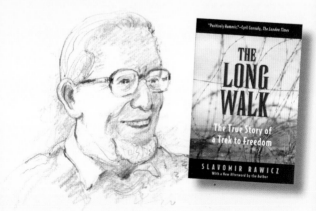

His story has been the subject of controversy since it was turned into the book 'The Long Walk' in 1955. After the war he settled in Sandiacre and taught handicrafts. Obviously he'd had enough excitement.

291. The first number plate in Nottingham was AU1, registered by William Enfield Dowson in 1903. It featured in the James Bond film 'Goldfinger' on Goldfinger's own Rolls Royce, but it did so without the permission of the then owner and without any payment being made. AU2 was purchased by Police Surgeon Dr H. Owen Taylor from Cripps Garage on Arkwright Street, and AU3 was owned by cigarette magnate W.G. Player and registered in Lenton.

292. Kitty Hudson, born in Arnold in 1765, was a human pincushion. Inevitably, during the course of holding them in her mouth she swallowed a few – which led to several trips to the hospital for surgery. It didn't seem to do her too much harm though as she married and had 19 children.

293. Nottingham's richest man in the 18th century was textile magnate William Elliott, who lived and worked in the Brewhouse Yard under Castle Rock below Nottingham Castle. His vast wealth came from a secret recipe for black dye that gentlemen used on their stockings to show off their legs.

294. At 53, former Nottingham High School teacher Rev. Theodore Hardy (1863–1918) became one of the oldest awardees of the Victoria Cross, and was also one of the most decorated non-combatants of the First World War. He was a Padre in the Army Chaplains' Department attached to the Lincolnshire Regiment. On one of several instances of bravery he went out to bring back a wounded soldier lying ten feet from a German pillbox.

295. In July 1956, Transport Minister John Profumo chose Nottingham to host the inaugural commuter helicopter service, to operate between Nottingham and Leicester. It was run by BEA from a site in Lenton, and the fare to Leicester was 11 shillings single or £1 return. It was believed at the time that all Britain's major cities would be linked by helicopter by the mid-sixties, but due to operating costs and the Suez fuel crisis the service was suspended in November and never resumed.

296. Erasmus Darwin (1731–1802), grandfather of Charles Darwin was born at Elston Hall near Newark. He was a remarkable mind in his own right being a recognised physiologist, physician, philosopher, inventor and poet. During his lifetime he designed a rocket engine, drew up workable plans for canal locks, sewerage disposal and carriage suspension and even invented a speaking robot.

ERASMUS DARWIN
1731 - 1802
Born and lived at Elston Hall
1731 - 1756
Fellow of The Royal Society
1761 - 1802
Eminent Medical Doctor
Scientific Genius
Originator of The Biological Theory of Evolution
Leading Poet with the gift of friendship

Died at Breadsall Priory
near Derby

297. The Reverend William Mompesson was rector of the village of Eyam when it was hit by the plague in 1665. Though he boldly attempted to isolate the village he ultimately carried the stigma of the plague with him, and his next parish Eakring, forced him to live in a hut in Rufford Park for fear of infection. He also preached in the open air under a tree which became known as the Pulpit Ash. He is buried and commemorated in Eakring Church.

E.L.S. No. 2. William Mompesson, Rector of Eyam during the Plague.

JOHN DANIEL died NOTTINGHAMSHIRE NORFOLDEST ANNO [...]

1639-1709   PLAGUE PRIEST   EAKRING 2009

...RING 1709   St ANDREWS CHURCH

298. John Hartman from Sherwood was Chief Censor at Spandau Prison from 1953 to 1972. He had the task of reading every letter written by Rudolf Hess, who for much of that time was the only inmate in the prison. The pair met once a week for 19 years. Hartman went on to become the chief German interpreter with the Foreign Office in Berlin retiring in 1972. Hess died in Spandau Prison in 1987.

299. Baronet Sir Thomas Parkyn (1662–1741) was an eccentric resident of Bunny Hall. His hobbies ranged from amateur architect to physician to wrestling his staff (to which there is a monument in nearby St. Mary's churchyard). He wrote a book on 'Cornish Hugg Wrestling' and also kept two professionals on-hand at Bunny Hall. He also collected stone coffins!

300. Harry Wheatcroft (1898-1977) an eccentric rose grower and local character was born in Handel Street, Sneinton. He had a great gift for publicity, and his left-wing views led to him attending the May Day Parade in Moscow's Red Square. His niece, Anna Wheatcroft, married Tom Baker who went on to become Doctor Who.

301. Admiral Richard Howe (1726–1799), 1st Earl Howe of Langar, was the victor at the famous naval Battle of Ushant in 1794, known as 'The Glorious First of June', during which he captured seven French ships of the line. Because of his swarthy complextion he was known as 'Black Dick'.

Lord Howe's Nottingham townhouse, built in 1755, can be seen on the corner of Castle Gate and Stanford Street. In 1789, the house was occupied by a Mr Stanford who was a great royalist. He celebrated George III regaining his mental health by having the house redecorated.

Nottingham Castle

Acknowledgements

With special thanks to the following people and
organisations who made this book possible:

*Stewart Adams, Catherine McManus, Chris
Booth, Alison Hancock, Chris Slade, Phil Gillborn,
Graham Drury, Nottingham Evening Post
Publications, BBC Radio Nottingham, John Holmes,
Nottingham City Council, The Sunday Times, Left
Lion Magazine, Roland Hoggard, Miss Nancy
Harrison, Mr. 'Vacuum Cleaner' James Brown,
Brackenhurst College, Bromley House Library,
Gedling Church, Temple Printers, Weavers Wine
Merchants, Eastwood Library, Nottingham Boat
Club, Wollaton Park Industrial Museum, Broadway
Cinema, Nottingham Playhouse, The Nottingham
Club, Bestwood Lodge, Harby Church, Pendine
House, Dewdrop Inn Ilkeston, Sankey Ltd., Car
Colston Village, Thrumpton Hall, Thoresby Hall,
Elston Church, Eakring Church, Oxton Church, East
Stoke Church, Clumber Park, Park Estate, Bell Inn,
Dovecote Inn.*

*Design, artwork, illustrations, photography and cartoons
by Robert Bealby
www.artcentregraphics.co.uk*

Green's Mill Sneinton (fact 195)

Published by Gift of the GAB Publishing